A WHO HQ GRAPHIC NOVEL

Who the Man in the Air?

MICHAEL JORDAN

T0011404

To Caleb and Felix. Always go hard in the paint, fellas—GS

For my cousins. Especially Kordaryl Thomas,
the biggest basketball fan ever—BW

PENGUIN WORKSHOP
An imprint of Penguin Random House LLC, New York

First published in the United States of America by Penguin Workshop,
an imprint of Penguin Random House LLC, New York, 2022

Visit us online at penguinrandomhouse.com.

Library of Congress Cataloging-in-Publication Data is available.

Manufactured in Italy

ISBN 9780593385913 (pbk)   10 9 8 7 6 5 4 3 2   LEG
ISBN 9780593385920 (hc)   10 9 8 7 6 5 4 3 2 1 LEG

Lettering by Comicraft
Design by Mary Claire Cruz

This is a work of nonfiction. All of the events that unfold in the narrative
are rooted in historical fact. Some dialogue and characters have been fictionalized
in order to illustrate or teach a historical point.

For more information about your favorite historical figures, places, and events,
please visit whohq.com.

A WHO HQ GRAPHIC NOVEL

Who Is the Man in the Air?

MICHAEL JORDAN

by Gabe Soria
illustrated by Brittney Williams

Penguin Workshop

Introduction

It's the summer of 1997, and American professional basketball team the Chicago Bulls are once again competing for the highest prize in basketball: the National Basketball Association (NBA) Finals championship. The Chicago Bulls are a team to be feared and respected—they are the defending champions of the NBA, and this year they are playing against the Utah Jazz to keep the title. The winner of four out of seven games will determine which team takes the ultimate honor, and right now, the Jazz and the Bulls are tied at two games each. The fifth game in the series is coming up, and the pressure is on the Bulls to win again. But the Bulls have a not-so-secret weapon on their side: team leader and shooting guard Michael Jordan.

Jordan has long been considered one of basketball's greatest players, from his beginning as a junior varsity player in high school to winning a championship with the University of North Carolina Tar Heels in college. Now, at the end of his twelfth season with the Bulls, he has a chance to win his fifth NBA championship with the team. What's more, Jordan is a star on and off the court: He has a signature athletic shoe, Air Jordans, with sportswear brand Nike and starred in the blockbuster movie *Space Jam* just a year prior.

The day of the fifth game in the heated competition has arrived, and everyone is buzzing with adrenaline. If the Bulls win this series, it will be their fifth title in six years. If the Jazz win, it will be their first-ever championship. But the Chicago Bulls have one very big problem: Michael Jordan isn't feeling so good.

8

9

10

11

12

GAME THREE! JUNE 6, 1997, DELTA CENTER, SALT LAKE CITY.

THE CHANT OF MVP FOR KARL MALONE RIGHT FROM THE START, ALTHOUGH THAT CAN DO FUNNY THINGS IN THE OPPOSITE WAY BECAUSE IT COULD ALSO FIRE UP NUMBER 23, MICHAEL JORDAN.

MALONE AGAIN!

YEAH, BABY!

CHICAGO BULLS 93

UTAH JAZZ 104

AND THEY'RE ON THEIR FEET! STANDING OVATION. THE UTAH JAZZ GET BACK INTO THE SERIES WITH A SOLID PERFORMANCE!

GAME FOUR! JUNE 8, 1997, DELTA CENTER, SALT LAKE CITY.

NBA Finals · Game 4

CHICAGO BULLS 18

UTAH JAZZ 23

UTAH TAKES THE LEAD!

MALONE TO STOCKTON FOR THREE!

Final Score:
Bulls 73 Jazz 78
2 - 2

BRYON RUSSELL MOVES TO THE HOOP AND THE UTAH JAZZ HAVE DEFEATED THE CHICAGO BULLS!! THE SERIES IS TIED AT TWO!!

AND THE QUESTION IS THIS...

14

Positions in Basketball

A professional basketball game is played in four twelve-minute quarters and divided into two halves. The games are played with five people on each team on the court. The positions are the power forward, the center, the point guard, the small forward, and the shooting guard, each with their own important role to play. THE CENTER is the focus of a lot of the action; centers are sometimes the biggest player on the team, and they use their size to get close to the basket and score. THE POINT GUARD focuses on defense against the other team, and their main job is to stop them from scoring. THE POWER FORWARD plays a role much like the center, focusing on offense, particularly rebounds from the basket after a player takes a shot, and facing off against very tall opponents. THE SMALL FORWARD is a versatile player who can play both offense and defense against players large and small. THE SHOOTING GUARD is the best scorer on the team, specializing in (but not limited to) making baskets from farther away.

1. Point Guard
2. Shooting Guard
3. Small Forward
4. Power Forward
5. Center

Scottie Pippen

Born on September 25, 1965, in Hamburg, Arkansas, Scottie Pippen loved to play football and basketball from an early age. He played basketball all throughout high school, leading his team to the state playoffs and earning top conference honors. But because he stood at just six feet one inch tall and weighed less than 150 pounds at the time, no college offered him a basketball scholarship. Eventually, Scottie was accepted to the University of Central Arkansas and ended up making the team as a walk-on (a player who becomes part of the team without being recruited beforehand). During his time in college, Pippen grew to six foot eight and became a top-level player—as well as a favorite among NBA scouts.

Drafted by the Seattle SuperSonics and traded to the Bulls in 1987, Scottie played the position of small forward alongside Michael Jordan in every one of the team's championship seasons the following decade and was crucial in shaping the unstoppable Bulls dynasty in the 1990s. He was considered to be the other leader of the Bulls, especially after Michael Jordan's first retirement from the team. Pippen also played on the 1992 Summer Olympics "Dream Team" in Barcelona where they won the gold medal.

22

25

THE BULLS LOCKER ROOM.

WHAT'S UP, MIKE?

Air Jordan

Athlete-endorsed athletic shoes are almost as old as professional sports itself. There's the Chuck Taylor, or "Chucks," that were made for and named after early semi-pro basketball player Chuck Taylor. There's also the Jack Purcell shoe, which is named after a Canadian badminton player, and many more. But the most groundbreaking and game-changing athlete shoe ever is arguably the Air Jordan, named after Michael Jordan. Designed for Michael's personal use in 1984, the next year, the shoe was first made available to the general public and was an immediate hit, generating massive sales and even some controversy because of how coveted and expensive they were. Today, the shoes known to many simply as "Jordans" continue to be one of the most popular athletic shoes around.

THIS IS A PAIR OF AIR JORDAN XIIs, THE SHOE THAT MICHAEL JORDAN WORE DURING GAME 5 OF THE 1997 NBA FINALS.

Karl Malone

The Chicago Bulls' path to victory in the 1997 NBA Finals was far from secure. Their opponents, the Utah Jazz (the team was originally based in New Orleans, hence the name) were the champions of the NBA Western Conference and were led by Karl Malone. The Louisiana-born power forward was known by the nickname "The Mailman," which he received while playing college basketball and referred to his ability to "deliver" points while under pressure. Malone began his NBA career with the Jazz in 1985. In the summer of 1992, Malone played alongside Michael Jordan, Scottie Pippen, and Jazz teammate John Stockton on the "Dream Team" in the 1992 Summer Olympics, winning a gold medal. In 1996, he returned to play on the Olympic team and once again earned top honors. Another player who is considered one of the greatest to ever play professional basketball, he eventually retired from the NBA in 2005 after almost twenty seasons on the courts.

GO!!! JAZZ

UTAH JAZZ FANS ARE IN A GOOD MOOD TONIGHT, AFTER THEIR TEAM HAS WON TWO GAMES STRAIGHT AND TAKEN A COMMANDING LEAD IN THE FIRST QUARTER OF GAME FIVE.

THE JAZZ BENCH IS IN A GOOD MOOD, TOO, BUT THEY KNOW THAT IT'S TOO EARLY TO COUNT ON **ANYTHING** IN THIS GAME. BUT THEY **DO** KNOW THAT THEY HAVE AN ADVANTAGE:

A SICK MICHAEL JORDAN, WHO ISN'T PLAYING ANYWHERE NEAR THE LEVEL WE'VE COME TO EXPECT FROM HIM. WE'LL SEE IF HE CAN GET IT TOGETHER IN THE NEXT QUARTER.

41

43

THIRD QUARTER.

NBA Finals · Game 5
CHICAGO BULLS 49
VS
UTAH JAZZ 53

THE BULLS' TRAINER SAYS THAT JORDAN IS EXHAUSTED, DEHYDRATED, AND A LITTLE BIT OUT OF IT. BUT HE'S STILL PLAYING.

45

FOURTH QUARTER.

AT THE BEGINNING OF THE FOURTH QUARTER HERE IN SALT LAKE CITY, THE BULLS TRAIL THE UTAH JAZZ...

NBA Finals · Game 5

CHICAGO BULLS 67

VS

UTAH JAZZ 72

BUT WAIT—JORDAN IS COMING **ALIVE!** THE BULLS ARE NOW ONLY SIX POINTS BEHIND, 77-71!

AND THAT THREE-POINTER TIES THE GAME, 77-77! AND HE DID IT IN CASUAL FORM—AND YOU COULD SEE HOW EXHAUSTED MICHAEL JORDAN IS.

BUT JORDAN IS BACK IN POSSESSION OF THE BALL WITH FORTY SECONDS REMAINING!

IT'S JORDAN TO PIPPEN...

AND PIPPEN BACK TO JORDAN, WHO GOES UP FOR THE THREE...

C'MON...

56

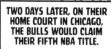

TWO DAYS LATER, ON THEIR HOME COURT IN CHICAGO, THE BULLS WOULD CLAIM THEIR FIFTH NBA TITLE.

Conclusion

After winning the fifth game in the 1997 NBA Finals, the Chicago Bulls and Michael Jordan went on to defeat the Utah Jazz in the next championship game on June 12, 1997, on their home court. Jordan would later be named the Most Valuable Player (MVP) of the series. The next year, the Bulls would face the Jazz again at the NBA Finals and would once again emerge victorious. Michael Jordan would win a total of six championship rings in his NBA career.

Jordan retired after that win, his second retirement from basketball. Three years later, he would return to the NBA, but this time to play with the Washington Wizards from 2001 to 2003, after which he retired for the third and final time. Though still a great player, Jordan's seasons with the Wizards never saw him achieve the heights he had with the Bulls. His championship win in 1998 would be his last, and his performance in Game Five of the 1997 NBA series—which would come to be known as "The Flu Game" despite the other theories about the origin of Jordan's sickness—would go down in history as one of the greatest ever played by one of the greatest—if not *the* greatest—basketball players in the sport.

Timeline of Michael Jordan's Life

1963	Born in Brooklyn, New York
1978	Becomes a junior varsity (and later varsity) player on the Emsley A. Laney High School basketball team
1982	Wins the NCAA basketball championship with the University of North Carolina Tar Heels
1984	Drafted by the Chicago Bulls
	Wins first Olympic gold medal at the Summer Games in Los Angeles
1991	Wins first NBA championship with the Bulls
1992	Wins second NBA championship with the Bulls
	Wins second gold medal as part of the "Dream Team" at the 1992 Olympics in Barcelona
1993	Wins third NBA championship with the Bulls and retires for the first time
1995	Rejoins the Bulls
1996	Wins fourth NBA championship with the Bulls
1997	Wins fifth NBA championship with the Bulls
1998	Wins sixth NBA championship with the Bulls and retires for the second time
2003	Retires from basketball for the third and final time

Bibliography

*Books for young readers

*Anderson, Kirsten. *Who Is Michael Jordan?* New York: Penguin Workshop, 2019.

*Christopher, Matt, with Glenn Stout and Stephanie Peters. *Legends in Sports: Michael Jordan*. New York: Little, Brown and Company, 1996.

Halberstam, David. *Playing for Keeps: Michael Jordan and the World He Made*. New York: Random House, 1999.

Hehir, Jason, dir. *The Last Dance*. 2020. Los Angeles: ESPN Films/Netflix, 2020, streaming.

Jordan, Michael. *Driven from Within*. New York: Atria Books, 2005.

Krugel, Mitchell. *Jordan: The Man, His Words, His Life*. New York: St. Martin's Press, 1994.

Lazenby, Roland. *Michael Jordan: The Life*. New York: Little, Brown and Company, 2014.

*Motin, Adam. *The Legend of Michael Jordan*. Chicago: Triumph Books, 2000.

Pytka, Joe, dir. *Space Jam*. 1996. Burbank: Warner Brothers, 2016, Blu-ray.

Santiago, Wilfred. *Michael Jordan: Bull on Parade*. Seattle: Fantagraphics, 2014.

Smith, Sam. *There Is No Next: NBA Legends on the Legacy of Michael Jordan*. New York: Diversion Publishing, 2014.

STEVE BURNS

Gabe Soria is best known in

the kidlit community for reinventing the choice-driven book genre with his four-book series, Midnight Arcade. He has also written several comic books for DC Comics, including *Batman '66*, and has collaborated with the Black Keys' Dan Auerbach on the *Murder Ballads* comic book.

Brittney Williams is a

Los Angeles-based creative originally from South Carolina. Williams is a storyboard and comic book artist who draws A LOT. In 2012, she interned at Walt Disney Animation Studios as a storyboard artist. Since then, she's worked for a variety of animation studios and publishers including Netflix, Cartoon Network, DreamWorks TV, BOOM! Studios, DC Comics, and Marvel Comics. As a two-time GLAAD award nominee, she exists to create things for kids and the queer community.